50 Gourmet Sandwich Recipes for Home

By: Kelly Johnson

Table of Contents

- Truffled Grilled Cheese with Balsamic Onions
- Lobster Roll with Lemon-Herb Mayo
- Fig and Prosciutto Panini with Brie
- Smoked Salmon Bagel Sandwich with Cream Cheese
- Roast Beef and Horseradish Aioli on Ciabatta
- Caprese Sandwich with Pesto Mayo
- Turkey, Cranberry, and Brie Croissant
- Grilled Vegetable Wrap with Hummus
- Tuna Nicoise Sandwich with Olive Tapenade
- Cuban Sandwich with Mojo-Marinated Pork
- Chicken Caesar Wrap with Garlic Croutons
- Pear, Blue Cheese, and Arugula Panini
- Roasted Eggplant and Red Pepper on Focaccia
- Roast Pork Banh Mi with Pickled Vegetables
- Reuben Sandwich with Russian Dressing
- Italian Submarine Sandwich with Genoa Salami
- Shrimp Po' Boy with Remoulade Sauce
- Mediterranean Veggie Sandwich with Sun-Dried Tomato Aioli
- Croque Monsieur with Gruyere and Ham
- Chicken Shawarma Pita with Garlic Sauce
- Portobello Mushroom and Goat Cheese Panini
- Smoked Turkey and Avocado on Sourdough
- Grilled Portobello and Red Pepper Wrap with Pesto
- Beef Tenderloin Slider with Horseradish Cream
- Smoked Gouda and Apple Butter on Multigrain Bread
- California Club Sandwich with Avocado and Bacon
- Pulled BBQ Jackfruit Sandwich with Slaw
- Pesto Chicken Salad Croissant
- Grilled Peach and Prosciutto on Baguette
- Spicy Tofu Banh Mi with Sriracha Mayo
- Roasted Vegetable and Goat Cheese Ciabatta
- BLT with Basil Mayo on Toasted Sourdough
- Crab Cake Sandwich with Old Bay Aioli
- Turkey Reuben with Coleslaw and Swiss Cheese
- Grilled Halloumi and Vegetable Wrap with Tzatziki

- Roast Beef and Gorgonzola on Rye
- Veggie Burger with Caramelized Onions and Smoked Gouda
- Chicken Gyro with Tzatziki Sauce
- Pear, Gouda, and Bacon Panini
- Smoked Salmon and Avocado Toasted Bagel
- Roast Lamb Sandwich with Mint Aioli
- Portobello Mushroom Reuben with Russian Dressing
- Grilled Chicken and Fig Jam on Brioche
- Buffalo Cauliflower Wrap with Blue Cheese Dressing
- Turkey and Cranberry Chutney on Walnut Bread
- Grilled Asparagus and Pesto Mayo on Sourdough
- Prosciutto, Fig, and Arugula on Baguette
- Smoked Salmon and Cucumber Tea Sandwiches
- Turkey, Apple, and Brie on Cranberry Walnut Bread
- Steak and Caramelized Onion Sandwich with Horseradish Cream

Truffled Grilled Cheese with Balsamic Onions

Ingredients:

- 4 slices of artisan bread (such as sourdough or ciabatta)
- 1 cup shredded truffle cheese (such as Gouda or Fontina)
- 1 large onion, thinly sliced
- 2 tablespoons balsamic vinegar
- 2 tablespoons olive oil
- Salt and pepper to taste
- Butter, softened, for spreading

Instructions:

1. Heat olive oil in a skillet over medium heat. Add the sliced onions and sauté until they start to soften, about 5 minutes.
2. Reduce the heat to low and continue cooking the onions, stirring occasionally, until they are caramelized and golden brown, about 20-25 minutes.
3. Stir in the balsamic vinegar and cook for an additional 2-3 minutes, until the vinegar has evaporated. Season with salt and pepper to taste. Remove from heat and set aside.
4. Spread softened butter on one side of each slice of bread.
5. Place one slice of bread, buttered side down, on a clean surface. Sprinkle half of the shredded truffle cheese on top.
6. Spoon half of the caramelized onions over the cheese, then sprinkle the remaining cheese on top.
7. Place the second slice of bread on top, buttered side facing up.
8. Heat a skillet or griddle over medium heat. Carefully transfer the assembled sandwich to the skillet.
9. Cook for 3-4 minutes on each side, or until the bread is golden brown and the cheese is melted.
10. Remove from the skillet and let cool for a minute or two before slicing.
11. Serve hot and enjoy the luxurious flavors of truffled grilled cheese with balsamic onions!

Lobster Roll with Lemon-Herb Mayo

Ingredients:

For the Lemon-Herb Mayo:

- 1/2 cup mayonnaise
- Zest of 1 lemon
- 1 tablespoon fresh lemon juice
- 1 tablespoon chopped fresh parsley
- 1 tablespoon chopped fresh chives
- Salt and pepper to taste

For the Lobster Roll:

- 1 lb cooked lobster meat, chopped into bite-sized pieces
- 4-6 split-top hot dog buns or brioche rolls
- 2 tablespoons unsalted butter, melted
- Chopped fresh chives for garnish (optional)
- Lemon wedges for serving

Instructions:

1. In a small bowl, whisk together the mayonnaise, lemon zest, lemon juice, chopped parsley, chopped chives, salt, and pepper until well combined. Adjust seasoning to taste. Set aside in the refrigerator while you prepare the lobster.
2. In a large mixing bowl, combine the chopped lobster meat with the prepared lemon-herb mayo. Gently toss until the lobster meat is evenly coated with the mayo mixture. Refrigerate the lobster salad while you prepare the buns.
3. Preheat a skillet or griddle over medium heat. Brush the split-top buns or brioche rolls with melted butter on the cut sides.
4. Place the buns on the preheated skillet or griddle, cut-side down. Toast until golden brown and lightly crispy, about 2-3 minutes.
5. Remove the toasted buns from the skillet and divide the chilled lobster salad among them, filling each bun generously with the lobster mixture.
6. Sprinkle with additional chopped chives for garnish, if desired. Serve the lobster rolls immediately with lemon wedges on the side.
7. Enjoy your homemade Lobster Rolls with Lemon-Herb Mayo, a taste of seaside indulgence!

Fig and Prosciutto Panini with Brie

Ingredients:

- 8 slices of sourdough bread
- 8 slices of prosciutto
- 8 oz brie cheese, thinly sliced
- 1/2 cup fig preserves
- 1 cup fresh arugula
- Butter, softened, for spreading

Instructions:

1. Preheat a panini press or grill pan over medium heat.
2. Take two slices of sourdough bread and spread fig preserves on one side of each slice.
3. Layer prosciutto slices on top of the fig preserves on one slice of bread.
4. Place thinly sliced brie cheese on top of the prosciutto.
5. Add a handful of fresh arugula on top of the brie.
6. Place the other slice of bread, fig side down, on top to form a sandwich.
7. Spread softened butter on the outer sides of the sandwich.
8. Place the sandwich in the preheated panini press or grill pan. If using a grill pan, place another heavy pan on top of the sandwich to press it down.
9. Cook the sandwich for 3-4 minutes on each side, or until the bread is golden brown and crispy, and the cheese is melted.
10. Remove the sandwich from the panini press or grill pan and let it cool for a minute.
11. Slice the Fig and Prosciutto Panini with Brie diagonally and serve warm.
12. Enjoy the delicious combination of sweet figs, salty prosciutto, creamy brie, and peppery arugula in this gourmet grilled sandwich!

Smoked Salmon Bagel Sandwich with Cream Cheese

Ingredients:

- 2 bagels, sliced and toasted
- 4 oz smoked salmon
- 4 oz cream cheese
- 1 tablespoon capers
- 1 small red onion, thinly sliced
- 1 tomato, sliced
- Fresh dill, for garnish (optional)
- Lemon wedges, for serving

Instructions:

1. Spread a generous amount of cream cheese on each half of the toasted bagels.
2. Layer the smoked salmon on the bottom half of each bagel.
3. Sprinkle capers evenly over the smoked salmon.
4. Top with thinly sliced red onion and tomato slices.
5. Garnish with fresh dill, if desired.
6. Close the sandwiches with the top halves of the bagels.
7. Serve the smoked salmon bagel sandwiches immediately, with lemon wedges on the side for squeezing over the salmon.
8. Enjoy your delicious and satisfying Smoked Salmon Bagel Sandwiches with Cream Cheese for breakfast or brunch!

Roast Beef and Horseradish Aioli on Ciabatta

Ingredients:

- 1 lb thinly sliced roast beef
- 4 ciabatta rolls, sliced in half
- 1/2 cup mayonnaise
- 2 tablespoons prepared horseradish
- 1 tablespoon lemon juice
- 1 clove garlic, minced
- Salt and pepper to taste
- 1 cup arugula or baby spinach
- Optional: sliced red onion, tomato, or any other desired toppings

Instructions:

1. Preheat your oven to 350°F (175°C).
2. In a small bowl, mix together the mayonnaise, prepared horseradish, lemon juice, minced garlic, salt, and pepper to create the horseradish aioli. Adjust the amount of horseradish to your taste preference.
3. Spread a generous amount of the horseradish aioli onto the bottom half of each ciabatta roll.
4. Layer the thinly sliced roast beef on top of the aioli.
5. Add a handful of arugula or baby spinach on top of the roast beef.
6. If desired, add any additional toppings such as sliced red onion or tomato.
7. Close the sandwiches with the top halves of the ciabatta rolls.
8. Place the assembled sandwiches on a baking sheet and bake in the preheated oven for about 5-7 minutes, or until the bread is lightly toasted and the roast beef is warmed through.
9. Remove from the oven and serve immediately.
10. Enjoy your flavorful Roast Beef and Horseradish Aioli sandwiches on ciabatta rolls!

Caprese Sandwich with Pesto Mayo

Ingredients:

- 4 ciabatta rolls, sliced in half
- 2 large ripe tomatoes, thinly sliced
- 8 oz fresh mozzarella cheese, sliced
- 1/2 cup fresh basil leaves
- 1/4 cup mayonnaise
- 2 tablespoons prepared pesto
- Salt and pepper to taste
- Optional: Balsamic glaze for drizzling

Instructions:

1. In a small bowl, mix together the mayonnaise and prepared pesto until well combined. Taste and adjust the amount of pesto to your liking. Set aside.
2. Slice the ciabatta rolls in half horizontally to create the top and bottom halves of the sandwich.
3. Spread a generous amount of the pesto mayo onto the bottom half of each ciabatta roll.
4. Layer thinly sliced tomatoes on top of the pesto mayo.
5. Place slices of fresh mozzarella cheese on top of the tomatoes.
6. Season the mozzarella with a pinch of salt and pepper.
7. Arrange fresh basil leaves on top of the mozzarella cheese.
8. Optional: Drizzle a little balsamic glaze over the basil leaves for extra flavor.
9. Close the sandwiches with the top halves of the ciabatta rolls.
10. Serve the Caprese Sandwiches with Pesto Mayo immediately, or wrap them tightly in foil or parchment paper for a picnic or on-the-go meal.
11. Enjoy the delicious combination of flavors in this Caprese Sandwich with Pesto Mayo!

Turkey, Cranberry, and Brie Croissant

Ingredients:

- 4 croissants, sliced in half
- 8 slices of cooked turkey breast
- 4 oz Brie cheese, thinly sliced
- 1/2 cup cranberry sauce (homemade or store-bought)
- 1/4 cup baby spinach or arugula leaves
- 2 tablespoons Dijon mustard (optional)
- Butter, softened, for spreading

Instructions:

1. Preheat your oven to 350°F (175°C).
2. Slice the croissants in half horizontally to create the top and bottom halves of the sandwich.
3. If desired, spread a thin layer of Dijon mustard on the bottom half of each croissant.
4. Layer slices of cooked turkey breast on top of the mustard.
5. Place thinly sliced Brie cheese on top of the turkey.
6. Spoon cranberry sauce over the Brie cheese layer.
7. Add a handful of baby spinach or arugula leaves on top of the cranberry sauce.
8. Close the sandwiches with the top halves of the croissants.
9. Spread a little softened butter on the outside of each croissant.
10. Place the assembled croissant sandwiches on a baking sheet lined with parchment paper.
11. Bake in the preheated oven for about 5-7 minutes, or until the croissants are warm and lightly toasted, and the cheese is melted.
12. Remove from the oven and let cool for a minute before serving.
13. Enjoy your delicious Turkey, Cranberry, and Brie Croissant sandwiches warm from the oven!

Grilled Vegetable Wrap with Hummus

Ingredients:

- 4 large whole wheat or spinach tortillas
- 1 zucchini, sliced lengthwise
- 1 yellow squash, sliced lengthwise
- 1 red bell pepper, sliced into strips
- 1 yellow bell pepper, sliced into strips
- 1 small red onion, sliced into rings
- 1 cup cherry tomatoes, halved
- 1 tablespoon olive oil
- Salt and pepper to taste
- 1 cup hummus (homemade or store-bought)
- Handful of baby spinach or arugula leaves
- Optional: crumbled feta cheese, sliced avocado, chopped fresh herbs (such as parsley or cilantro)

Instructions:

1. Preheat a grill or grill pan over medium heat.
2. In a large bowl, toss the sliced zucchini, yellow squash, bell peppers, red onion, and cherry tomatoes with olive oil, salt, and pepper until evenly coated.
3. Place the vegetables on the preheated grill and cook for 3-4 minutes per side, or until they are tender and have grill marks. Remove from the grill and set aside.
4. Warm the tortillas slightly in the microwave or on a clean, dry skillet for about 10-15 seconds to make them more pliable.
5. Spread a generous layer of hummus onto each tortilla, leaving a border around the edges.
6. Arrange a handful of baby spinach or arugula leaves on top of the hummus.
7. Place some of the grilled vegetables on top of the greens.
8. Optional: Sprinkle crumbled feta cheese, add sliced avocado, or sprinkle with chopped fresh herbs for extra flavor.
9. Fold the sides of the tortilla inwards, then roll it up tightly from the bottom to enclose the filling.
10. Repeat with the remaining tortillas and filling ingredients.
11. Slice the wraps in half diagonally before serving, if desired.
12. Serve the Grilled Vegetable Wraps with Hummus immediately, or wrap them tightly in foil or parchment paper for a picnic or on-the-go meal.
13. Enjoy your delicious and nutritious Grilled Vegetable Wraps with Hummus!

Tuna Nicoise Sandwich with Olive Tapenade

Ingredients:

For the Olive Tapenade:

- 1 cup pitted black olives (such as Kalamata), drained
- 2 tablespoons capers, drained
- 2 cloves garlic, minced
- 2 tablespoons fresh lemon juice
- 2 tablespoons extra virgin olive oil
- Salt and pepper to taste

For the Tuna Nicoise Sandwich:

- 4 ciabatta rolls or baguettes, sliced in half
- 2 cans (5 oz each) of tuna, drained
- 4 hard-boiled eggs, sliced
- 1 cup cherry tomatoes, halved
- 1/2 cup green beans, blanched and sliced
- 1/4 cup red onion, thinly sliced
- 1/4 cup fresh parsley or basil leaves
- Olive Tapenade (from the above ingredients)
- Salt and pepper to taste

Instructions:

1. To make the Olive Tapenade, combine the pitted black olives, capers, minced garlic, lemon juice, and extra virgin olive oil in a food processor. Pulse until the mixture forms a coarse paste. Season with salt and pepper to taste. Set aside.
2. Preheat a grill or grill pan over medium heat.
3. Place the sliced ciabatta rolls or baguettes on the grill and toast them for about 2-3 minutes on each side, until lightly golden and crispy. Remove from the grill and set aside.
4. In a mixing bowl, combine the drained tuna with a few tablespoons of the Olive Tapenade. Mix well to combine.
5. To assemble the sandwiches, spread a generous layer of the remaining Olive Tapenade on the bottom halves of the grilled ciabatta rolls or baguettes.
6. Top with the tuna mixture, sliced hard-boiled eggs, halved cherry tomatoes, sliced green beans, red onion slices, and fresh parsley or basil leaves.
7. Season with salt and pepper to taste.

8. Place the top halves of the ciabatta rolls or baguettes on top of the sandwich fillings to form sandwiches.
9. Serve the Tuna Nicoise Sandwiches immediately, or wrap them tightly in foil or parchment paper for a picnic or on-the-go meal.
10. Enjoy your delicious and satisfying Tuna Nicoise Sandwiches with Olive Tapenade!

Cuban Sandwich with Mojo-Marinated Pork

Ingredients:

For the Mojo-Marinated Pork:

- 1 lb pork tenderloin or pork shoulder, thinly sliced
- 1/4 cup orange juice
- 1/4 cup lime juice
- 4 cloves garlic, minced
- 2 tablespoons olive oil
- 1 teaspoon ground cumin
- 1 teaspoon dried oregano
- Salt and pepper to taste

For the Cuban Sandwich:

- 4 Cuban bread rolls or hoagie rolls, sliced in half
- Mojo-Marinated Pork (from the above ingredients)
- 8 slices Swiss cheese
- 8 slices ham
- 1 cup dill pickles, thinly sliced
- Yellow mustard, to taste
- Butter, softened, for spreading

Instructions:

1. In a bowl, whisk together the orange juice, lime juice, minced garlic, olive oil, ground cumin, dried oregano, salt, and pepper to make the marinade.
2. Place the thinly sliced pork in a shallow dish or resealable plastic bag. Pour the marinade over the pork, making sure it is well coated. Cover and refrigerate for at least 2 hours, or preferably overnight, to marinate.
3. Preheat a grill or grill pan over medium-high heat.
4. Remove the pork from the marinade and discard the excess marinade. Grill the pork slices for 3-4 minutes on each side, or until cooked through and slightly charred. Remove from the grill and set aside.
5. Preheat a panini press or grill pan over medium heat.
6. Spread a thin layer of mustard on the bottom halves of each Cuban bread roll or hoagie roll.
7. Layer sliced ham, grilled mojo-marinated pork, Swiss cheese, and dill pickle slices on top of the mustard.

8. Close the sandwiches with the top halves of the Cuban bread rolls or hoagie rolls.
9. Spread a little softened butter on the outside of each sandwich.
10. Place the sandwiches on the preheated panini press or grill pan. If using a grill pan, place another heavy pan on top of the sandwiches to press them down.
11. Cook for 3-4 minutes on each side, or until the bread is golden brown and crispy, and the cheese is melted.
12. Remove from the panini press or grill pan and let cool for a minute before serving.
13. Slice the Cuban Sandwiches diagonally and serve warm.
14. Enjoy your delicious and flavorful Cuban Sandwiches with Mojo-Marinated Pork!

Chicken Caesar Wrap with Garlic Croutons

Ingredients:

For the Garlic Croutons:

- 2 cups cubed bread (such as French bread or ciabatta)
- 2 tablespoons olive oil
- 2 cloves garlic, minced
- Salt and pepper to taste

For the Chicken Caesar Wrap:

- 4 large flour tortillas or wraps
- 2 cups cooked chicken breast, sliced or shredded
- 1 cup romaine lettuce, chopped
- 1/4 cup grated Parmesan cheese
- 1/4 cup Caesar dressing (homemade or store-bought)
- Garlic Croutons (from the above ingredients)
- Salt and pepper to taste

Instructions:

1. Preheat the oven to 375°F (190°C).
2. In a mixing bowl, toss the cubed bread with olive oil, minced garlic, salt, and pepper until evenly coated.
3. Spread the seasoned bread cubes in a single layer on a baking sheet.
4. Bake in the preheated oven for 10-15 minutes, or until the croutons are golden brown and crispy. Remove from the oven and set aside.
5. To assemble the Chicken Caesar Wraps, lay out the flour tortillas or wraps on a clean surface.
6. Divide the cooked chicken breast slices or shredded chicken evenly among the tortillas, placing the chicken in the center of each wrap.
7. Top the chicken with chopped romaine lettuce, grated Parmesan cheese, and a handful of garlic croutons.
8. Drizzle Caesar dressing over the ingredients on each wrap.
9. Season with salt and pepper to taste.
10. Fold in the sides of each tortilla and roll them up tightly to form wraps.
11. Slice the wraps in half diagonally before serving, if desired.
12. Serve the Chicken Caesar Wraps immediately, or wrap them tightly in foil or parchment paper for a picnic or on-the-go meal.

13. Enjoy your delicious and satisfying Chicken Caesar Wraps with Garlic Croutons!

Pear, Blue Cheese, and Arugula Panini

Ingredients:

- 8 slices of sourdough bread
- 2 ripe pears, thinly sliced
- 4 oz blue cheese, crumbled
- 2 cups baby arugula leaves
- 2 tablespoons honey
- Butter, softened, for spreading

Instructions:

1. Preheat a panini press or grill pan over medium heat.
2. Lay out the slices of sourdough bread on a clean surface.
3. Divide the thinly sliced pears evenly among 4 slices of the bread.
4. Sprinkle crumbled blue cheese over the pears on each slice.
5. Top the blue cheese and pear with a handful of baby arugula leaves.
6. Drizzle a little honey over the arugula on each slice.
7. Place the remaining slices of bread on top to form sandwiches.
8. Spread softened butter on the outer sides of each sandwich.
9. Place the sandwiches in the preheated panini press or grill pan.
10. Cook for 3-4 minutes on each side, or until the bread is golden brown and crispy, and the cheese is melted.
11. Remove from the panini press or grill pan and let cool for a minute before serving.
12. Slice the Pear, Blue Cheese, and Arugula Panini in half diagonally before serving, if desired.
13. Serve the panini sandwiches warm and enjoy the delicious combination of flavors!

Roasted Eggplant and Red Pepper on Focaccia

Ingredients:

For the Roasted Vegetables:

- 1 large eggplant, sliced into rounds
- 2 red bell peppers, sliced into strips
- 2 tablespoons olive oil
- Salt and pepper to taste
- 2 cloves garlic, minced
- 1 teaspoon dried thyme

For the Focaccia:

- 1 loaf of focaccia bread, sliced horizontally
- 2 tablespoons olive oil
- 1 tablespoon balsamic vinegar
- 1 cup baby spinach or arugula leaves
- 4 oz goat cheese, crumbled (optional)
- Fresh basil leaves for garnish (optional)

Instructions:

1. Preheat the oven to 425°F (220°C).
2. Place the sliced eggplant and red bell peppers on a baking sheet lined with parchment paper.
3. Drizzle the olive oil over the vegetables and toss to coat evenly. Season with salt, pepper, minced garlic, and dried thyme.
4. Roast the vegetables in the preheated oven for 20-25 minutes, or until they are tender and slightly caramelized. Remove from the oven and set aside.
5. While the vegetables are roasting, prepare the focaccia. Brush the cut sides of the focaccia bread with olive oil and balsamic vinegar.
6. Place the focaccia bread on a baking sheet and toast in the oven for 5-7 minutes, or until lightly golden and crispy.
7. Remove the toasted focaccia from the oven and assemble the sandwiches. Layer the roasted eggplant and red bell peppers on the bottom half of the focaccia.
8. Top with baby spinach or arugula leaves and crumbled goat cheese, if using.
9. Place the top half of the focaccia over the fillings to form sandwiches.
10. Slice the sandwiches into individual portions and garnish with fresh basil leaves, if desired.

11. Serve the Roasted Eggplant and Red Pepper on Focaccia sandwiches warm and enjoy the delicious flavors!

Roast Pork Banh Mi with Pickled Vegetables

Ingredients:

For the Pickled Vegetables:

- 1 large carrot, julienned
- 1 daikon radish, julienned
- 1/2 cup rice vinegar
- 1/4 cup water
- 2 tablespoons sugar
- 1 teaspoon salt

For the Roast Pork:

- 1 lb pork tenderloin or pork shoulder, thinly sliced
- 2 tablespoons soy sauce
- 2 tablespoons hoisin sauce
- 1 tablespoon fish sauce
- 2 cloves garlic, minced
- 1 teaspoon five-spice powder
- 1 tablespoon vegetable oil

For the Banh Mi:

- Baguette or French rolls, sliced horizontally
- Mayonnaise
- Sriracha sauce (optional)
- Fresh cilantro leaves
- Thinly sliced cucumber
- Thinly sliced jalapeño peppers (optional)

Instructions:

1. Start by preparing the pickled vegetables. In a small saucepan, combine the rice vinegar, water, sugar, and salt. Heat over medium heat until the sugar and salt are dissolved. Remove from heat and let cool slightly.
2. Place the julienned carrots and daikon radish in a glass jar or bowl. Pour the pickling liquid over the vegetables, ensuring they are fully submerged. Cover and refrigerate for at least 1 hour, or overnight for best results.

3. In a bowl, combine the soy sauce, hoisin sauce, fish sauce, minced garlic, and five-spice powder to make the marinade for the roast pork. Add the thinly sliced pork and toss to coat evenly. Let marinate for at least 30 minutes.
4. Heat vegetable oil in a skillet or grill pan over medium-high heat. Add the marinated pork slices and cook for 2-3 minutes on each side, or until cooked through and caramelized. Remove from heat and set aside.
5. Slice the baguette or French rolls horizontally and spread a generous amount of mayonnaise on one side of each slice. If desired, drizzle sriracha sauce over the mayonnaise for added heat.
6. Layer the cooked roast pork slices on the bottom halves of the baguette or French rolls.
7. Top the pork with pickled vegetables, fresh cilantro leaves, thinly sliced cucumber, and thinly sliced jalapeño peppers, if using.
8. Place the top halves of the baguette or French rolls over the fillings to form sandwiches.
9. Slice the sandwiches into individual portions and serve immediately.
10. Enjoy your delicious and flavorful Roast Pork Banh Mi with Pickled Vegetables!

Reuben Sandwich with Russian Dressing

Ingredients:

For the Russian Dressing:

- 1/2 cup mayonnaise
- 2 tablespoons ketchup
- 1 tablespoon sweet pickle relish
- 1 teaspoon Worcestershire sauce
- 1 teaspoon hot sauce (such as Tabasco)
- 1 teaspoon lemon juice
- Salt and pepper to taste

For the Reuben Sandwich:

- 8 slices of rye bread
- 1 lb thinly sliced corned beef
- 8 slices Swiss cheese
- 1 cup sauerkraut, drained
- Russian Dressing (from the above ingredients)
- Butter, softened, for spreading

Instructions:

1. To make the Russian Dressing, combine the mayonnaise, ketchup, sweet pickle relish, Worcestershire sauce, hot sauce, lemon juice, salt, and pepper in a bowl. Mix well until all ingredients are thoroughly combined. Taste and adjust seasoning if needed. Set aside.
2. Preheat a skillet or griddle over medium heat.
3. Lay out the slices of rye bread on a clean surface.
4. Spread a generous amount of Russian dressing on one side of each slice of bread.
5. Layer thinly sliced corned beef on four of the slices of bread.
6. Top the corned beef with Swiss cheese slices.
7. Spread sauerkraut over the Swiss cheese on each sandwich.
8. Place the remaining slices of rye bread on top to form sandwiches, dressing side down.
9. Spread softened butter on the outer sides of each sandwich.
10. Place the sandwiches in the preheated skillet or griddle.

11. Cook for 3-4 minutes on each side, or until the bread is golden brown and crispy, and the cheese is melted.
12. Remove from the skillet or griddle and let cool for a minute before serving.
13. Slice the Reuben Sandwiches diagonally and serve hot.
14. Enjoy your classic and delicious Reuben Sandwiches with Russian Dressing!

Italian Submarine Sandwich with Genoa Salami

Ingredients:

For the Sandwich:

- 1 large Italian submarine roll or baguette, sliced lengthwise
- 1/4 lb sliced Genoa salami
- 1/4 lb sliced ham
- 1/4 lb sliced provolone cheese
- 1/4 lb sliced mortadella
- 1/4 lb sliced pepperoni
- 1/2 cup sliced black olives
- 1/2 cup sliced banana peppers
- 1/2 cup shredded iceberg lettuce
- 1 large tomato, sliced
- Salt and pepper to taste
- Olive oil and red wine vinegar for drizzling

For the Italian Dressing:

- 1/4 cup extra virgin olive oil
- 2 tablespoons red wine vinegar
- 1 clove garlic, minced
- 1 teaspoon dried oregano
- 1/2 teaspoon dried basil
- Salt and pepper to taste

Instructions:

1. Preheat the oven to 350°F (175°C).
2. Place the submarine roll or baguette on a baking sheet.
3. Layer the sliced Genoa salami, ham, provolone cheese, mortadella, and pepperoni on the bottom half of the roll.
4. Add sliced black olives and banana peppers on top of the meats and cheese.
5. Place the baking sheet in the oven and bake for about 5-7 minutes, or until the cheese is melted and the bread is slightly toasted.
6. While the sandwich is baking, prepare the Italian dressing. In a small bowl, whisk together the olive oil, red wine vinegar, minced garlic, dried oregano, dried basil, salt, and pepper until well combined.

7. Remove the sandwich from the oven and top with shredded iceberg lettuce and sliced tomatoes.
8. Drizzle the Italian dressing over the top of the sandwich.
9. Season with salt and pepper to taste.
10. Close the sandwich with the top half of the roll.
11. Slice the Italian Submarine Sandwich into individual portions and serve.
12. Enjoy your delicious and hearty Italian Submarine Sandwich with Genoa Salami!

Shrimp Po' Boy with Remoulade Sauce

Ingredients:

For the Remoulade Sauce:

- 1/2 cup mayonnaise
- 2 tablespoons Dijon mustard
- 1 tablespoon prepared horseradish
- 1 tablespoon hot sauce (such as Tabasco)
- 1 tablespoon lemon juice
- 2 cloves garlic, minced
- 1 teaspoon paprika
- 1 teaspoon Worcestershire sauce
- Salt and pepper to taste

For the Shrimp:

- 1 lb large shrimp, peeled and deveined
- 1 cup all-purpose flour
- 1 teaspoon paprika
- 1 teaspoon garlic powder
- Salt and pepper to taste
- Vegetable oil for frying

For the Po' Boy:

- 4 submarine rolls or French bread loaves, sliced lengthwise
- Shrimp (from the above ingredients)
- Remoulade sauce (from the above ingredients)
- Shredded lettuce
- Sliced tomatoes
- Sliced pickles
- Sliced red onion (optional)
- Lemon wedges for serving

Instructions:

1. To make the Remoulade Sauce, in a small bowl, whisk together the mayonnaise, Dijon mustard, prepared horseradish, hot sauce, lemon juice, minced garlic,

paprika, Worcestershire sauce, salt, and pepper until well combined. Cover and refrigerate until ready to use.
2. In a shallow dish, combine the all-purpose flour, paprika, garlic powder, salt, and pepper. Mix well.
3. Dredge the peeled and deveined shrimp in the seasoned flour mixture, shaking off any excess.
4. Heat vegetable oil in a large skillet or deep fryer to 350°F (175°C).
5. Fry the coated shrimp in batches for 2-3 minutes, or until golden brown and crispy. Remove from the oil using a slotted spoon and drain on paper towels.
6. To assemble the Po' Boy sandwiches, spread a generous amount of the prepared Remoulade sauce on the bottom half of each submarine roll or French bread loaf.
7. Layer shredded lettuce, sliced tomatoes, pickles, and sliced red onion (if using) on top of the Remoulade sauce.
8. Arrange the fried shrimp on top of the vegetables.
9. Close the sandwiches with the top halves of the rolls.
10. Serve the Shrimp Po' Boy sandwiches immediately, accompanied by lemon wedges for squeezing over the shrimp.
11. Enjoy your delicious and flavorful Shrimp Po' Boy with Remoulade Sauce!

Mediterranean Veggie Sandwich with Sun-Dried Tomato Aioli

Ingredients:

For the Sun-Dried Tomato Aioli:

- 1/2 cup mayonnaise
- 2 tablespoons sun-dried tomatoes, chopped
- 1 clove garlic, minced
- 1 tablespoon lemon juice
- Salt and pepper to taste

For the Sandwich:

- 4 ciabatta rolls or sandwich rolls, sliced in half
- 1 large eggplant, sliced into rounds
- 1 large zucchini, sliced into rounds
- 1 large red bell pepper, sliced into strips
- 1/4 cup olive oil
- Salt and pepper to taste
- 1 cup baby spinach or arugula leaves
- 1/2 cup crumbled feta cheese
- 1/4 cup sliced Kalamata olives
- Fresh basil leaves for garnish (optional)

Instructions:

1. Preheat the oven to 425°F (220°C).
2. In a small bowl, combine the mayonnaise, chopped sun-dried tomatoes, minced garlic, lemon juice, salt, and pepper to make the sun-dried tomato aioli. Mix well and set aside.
3. Place the sliced eggplant, zucchini, and red bell pepper on a baking sheet lined with parchment paper.
4. Drizzle olive oil over the vegetables and season with salt and pepper to taste. Toss to coat evenly.
5. Roast the vegetables in the preheated oven for 20-25 minutes, or until they are tender and slightly caramelized. Remove from the oven and let cool slightly.
6. To assemble the sandwiches, spread a generous amount of the sun-dried tomato aioli on the bottom half of each ciabatta roll or sandwich roll.
7. Layer roasted eggplant slices, zucchini slices, and red bell pepper strips on top of the aioli.

8. Top with baby spinach or arugula leaves, crumbled feta cheese, and sliced Kalamata olives.
9. Place the top halves of the ciabatta rolls or sandwich rolls over the fillings to form sandwiches.
10. Slice the sandwiches in half diagonally before serving, if desired.
11. Garnish with fresh basil leaves, if using.
12. Serve the Mediterranean Veggie Sandwiches with Sun-Dried Tomato Aioli immediately and enjoy!

This sandwich is packed with Mediterranean flavors and is perfect for a light and delicious meal.

Croque Monsieur with Gruyere and Ham

Ingredients:

For the Béchamel Sauce:

- 2 tablespoons unsalted butter
- 2 tablespoons all-purpose flour
- 1 cup milk
- 1/4 teaspoon nutmeg
- Salt and pepper to taste

For the Croque Monsieur:

- 8 slices of thick-cut bread (such as brioche or French bread)
- 4 tablespoons Dijon mustard
- 8 slices of ham
- 2 cups grated Gruyere cheese
- Béchamel sauce (from the above ingredients)
- Butter, softened, for spreading

Instructions:

1. To make the Béchamel Sauce, melt the butter in a saucepan over medium heat. Add the flour and whisk continuously until the mixture turns golden brown, about 2 minutes.
2. Gradually whisk in the milk, making sure there are no lumps. Cook the sauce, stirring constantly, until it thickens and coats the back of a spoon, about 5 minutes.
3. Stir in the nutmeg and season with salt and pepper to taste. Remove the saucepan from the heat and set aside.
4. Preheat a panini press or a large skillet over medium heat.
5. Spread Dijon mustard on one side of each slice of bread.
6. Place a slice of ham on top of the mustard on four of the slices of bread.
7. Sprinkle grated Gruyere cheese on top of the ham.
8. Spoon a generous amount of Béchamel sauce over the cheese layer on each sandwich.
9. Place the remaining slices of bread on top, mustard side down, to form sandwiches.
10. Spread softened butter on the outer sides of each sandwich.

11. Place the sandwiches on the preheated panini press or skillet. If using a skillet, press down on the sandwiches with a spatula to flatten slightly.
12. Cook the sandwiches for 3-4 minutes on each side, or until the bread is golden brown and crispy, and the cheese is melted.
13. Remove the sandwiches from the panini press or skillet and let cool for a minute before serving.
14. Slice the Croque Monsieur sandwiches diagonally and serve hot.
15. Enjoy your delicious and indulgent Croque Monsieur with Gruyere and Ham!

Chicken Shawarma Pita with Garlic Sauce

Ingredients:

For the Chicken Shawarma:

- 1 lb boneless, skinless chicken thighs, thinly sliced
- 2 cloves garlic, minced
- 2 teaspoons ground cumin
- 2 teaspoons ground coriander
- 1 teaspoon smoked paprika
- 1 teaspoon ground turmeric
- 1/2 teaspoon ground cinnamon
- 1/4 teaspoon cayenne pepper
- 2 tablespoons lemon juice
- 2 tablespoons olive oil
- Salt and pepper to taste

For the Garlic Sauce:

- 1/2 cup mayonnaise
- 2 cloves garlic, minced
- 1 tablespoon lemon juice
- Salt to taste

For Serving:

- Pita bread or flatbread
- Shredded lettuce
- Sliced tomatoes
- Sliced cucumbers
- Sliced red onions
- Fresh parsley or cilantro, chopped
- Pickles (optional)

Instructions:

1. In a bowl, combine the minced garlic, ground cumin, ground coriander, smoked paprika, ground turmeric, ground cinnamon, cayenne pepper, lemon juice, olive oil, salt, and pepper to make the marinade for the chicken shawarma.

2. Add the thinly sliced chicken thighs to the marinade and toss to coat evenly. Cover and refrigerate for at least 1 hour, or overnight for best results.
3. Preheat a grill or grill pan over medium-high heat.
4. Thread the marinated chicken slices onto skewers and grill for 4-5 minutes on each side, or until cooked through and slightly charred. Alternatively, you can cook the chicken in a skillet over medium-high heat until cooked through.
5. While the chicken is grilling, prepare the garlic sauce. In a small bowl, combine the mayonnaise, minced garlic, lemon juice, and salt. Mix well until smooth and creamy. Adjust seasoning to taste, if needed.
6. Warm the pita bread or flatbread in the oven or on a skillet.
7. To assemble the Chicken Shawarma Pitas, spread a generous amount of garlic sauce on each warmed pita bread.
8. Top with shredded lettuce, sliced tomatoes, sliced cucumbers, sliced red onions, grilled chicken shawarma, and chopped parsley or cilantro.
9. Add pickles if desired.
10. Roll up the pita bread tightly, tucking in the sides as you go.
11. Serve the Chicken Shawarma Pitas immediately, and enjoy!

This recipe captures the delicious flavors of traditional Middle Eastern chicken shawarma, and the creamy garlic sauce adds a delightful kick to each bite.

Portobello Mushroom and Goat Cheese Panini

Ingredients:

- 4 large portobello mushrooms, cleaned and sliced
- 2 tablespoons balsamic vinegar
- 2 tablespoons olive oil
- Salt and pepper to taste
- 4 ciabatta rolls or sandwich rolls, sliced in half
- 4 oz goat cheese, softened
- 1 cup baby spinach leaves
- 1 red bell pepper, roasted and sliced (optional)
- 1/4 cup caramelized onions (optional)
- 2 tablespoons pesto (optional)
- Butter, softened, for spreading

Instructions:

1. Preheat a grill pan or skillet over medium heat.
2. In a bowl, whisk together the balsamic vinegar, olive oil, salt, and pepper. Add the sliced portobello mushrooms and toss to coat evenly.
3. Place the marinated mushrooms on the preheated grill pan or skillet. Cook for 4-5 minutes on each side, or until tender and lightly charred. Remove from heat and set aside.
4. Spread softened goat cheese on the bottom half of each ciabatta roll or sandwich roll.
5. Layer grilled portobello mushrooms on top of the goat cheese.
6. Add baby spinach leaves, roasted red bell pepper slices, and caramelized onions if desired.
7. Spread pesto on the top halves of the ciabatta rolls or sandwich rolls.
8. Place the top halves of the rolls over the fillings to form sandwiches.
9. Spread softened butter on the outer sides of each sandwich.
10. Place the sandwiches on the preheated grill pan or skillet. If using a skillet, press down on the sandwiches with a spatula to flatten slightly.
11. Cook the sandwiches for 3-4 minutes on each side, or until the bread is golden brown and crispy, and the cheese is melted.
12. Remove the sandwiches from the grill pan or skillet and let cool for a minute before serving.
13. Slice the Portobello Mushroom and Goat Cheese Panini in half diagonally before serving, if desired.

14. Serve hot and enjoy the delicious combination of flavors!

Feel free to customize the panini with your favorite ingredients and toppings to suit your taste preferences.

Smoked Turkey and Avocado on Sourdough

Ingredients:

- 8 slices of sourdough bread
- 1/2 lb smoked turkey breast, thinly sliced
- 1 ripe avocado, sliced
- 1 cup mixed salad greens (such as arugula or spinach)
- 1 medium tomato, sliced
- 4 slices of Swiss cheese
- Salt and pepper to taste
- Dijon mustard (optional)
- Mayonnaise (optional)
- Butter, softened, for spreading

Instructions:

1. Preheat a skillet or grill pan over medium heat.
2. Lay out the slices of sourdough bread on a clean surface.
3. If desired, spread Dijon mustard or mayonnaise on one side of each slice of bread.
4. Layer smoked turkey slices on four slices of bread.
5. Top the turkey with avocado slices, mixed salad greens, tomato slices, and Swiss cheese slices.
6. Sprinkle salt and pepper to taste over the ingredients.
7. Place the remaining slices of bread on top to form sandwiches.
8. Spread softened butter on the outer sides of each sandwich.
9. Place the sandwiches in the preheated skillet or grill pan.
10. Cook for 3-4 minutes on each side, or until the bread is golden brown and crispy, and the cheese is melted.
11. Remove the sandwiches from the skillet or grill pan and let cool for a minute before serving.
12. Slice the Smoked Turkey and Avocado on Sourdough sandwiches diagonally before serving, if desired.
13. Serve hot and enjoy your delicious and satisfying meal!

Grilled Portobello and Red Pepper Wrap with Pesto

Ingredients:

For the Pesto:

- 2 cups fresh basil leaves, packed
- 1/2 cup grated Parmesan cheese
- 1/2 cup pine nuts or walnuts
- 3 cloves garlic, minced
- 1/2 cup extra virgin olive oil
- Salt and pepper to taste

For the Wrap:

- 4 large portobello mushrooms, cleaned and sliced
- 2 red bell peppers, sliced into strips
- 4 large flour tortillas or wraps
- Pesto (from the above ingredients)
- 1 cup baby spinach leaves
- 1/2 cup crumbled goat cheese or feta cheese (optional)
- Olive oil for grilling

Instructions:

1. To make the pesto, combine the basil leaves, grated Parmesan cheese, pine nuts or walnuts, and minced garlic in a food processor. Pulse until finely chopped.
2. With the food processor running, slowly drizzle in the olive oil until the pesto reaches your desired consistency. Season with salt and pepper to taste. Set aside.
3. Preheat a grill or grill pan over medium heat.
4. Brush the portobello mushroom slices and red pepper strips with olive oil and season with salt and pepper to taste.
5. Grill the portobello mushrooms for 3-4 minutes on each side, or until tender and slightly charred. Grill the red pepper strips for 2-3 minutes on each side, or until softened and slightly charred. Remove from the grill and set aside.
6. Warm the flour tortillas or wraps on the grill for 1-2 minutes on each side.
7. To assemble the wraps, spread a generous amount of pesto on each warmed tortilla or wrap.
8. Layer grilled portobello mushroom slices and red pepper strips on top of the pesto.

9. Add a handful of baby spinach leaves on top of the vegetables.
10. If using, sprinkle crumbled goat cheese or feta cheese over the spinach.
11. Roll up the tortillas or wraps tightly to form wraps.
12. Slice the wraps in half diagonally before serving, if desired.
13. Serve the Grilled Portobello and Red Pepper Wraps with Pesto immediately and enjoy!

These wraps are packed with flavor and make a delicious and satisfying meal. Feel free to customize the ingredients to suit your taste preferences.

Beef Tenderloin Slider with Horseradish Cream

Ingredients:

For the Beef Tenderloin:

- 1 lb beef tenderloin, trimmed and sliced into thin steaks
- Salt and pepper to taste
- 1 tablespoon olive oil

For the Horseradish Cream:

- 1/2 cup sour cream
- 2 tablespoons prepared horseradish
- 1 tablespoon Dijon mustard
- 1 tablespoon fresh lemon juice
- Salt and pepper to taste

For Serving:

- Mini slider buns or dinner rolls, sliced in half
- Baby arugula or lettuce leaves
- Sliced tomatoes
- Thinly sliced red onions
- Crispy fried onions (optional)
- Fresh parsley or chives for garnish (optional)

Instructions:

1. Preheat a grill or grill pan over high heat.
2. Season the beef tenderloin steaks with salt and pepper on both sides.
3. Drizzle olive oil over the steaks and rub to coat evenly.
4. Grill the beef tenderloin steaks for 2-3 minutes on each side, or until cooked to your desired doneness. Remove from the grill and let rest for a few minutes.
5. While the beef is grilling, prepare the horseradish cream. In a small bowl, mix together the sour cream, prepared horseradish, Dijon mustard, fresh lemon juice, salt, and pepper until well combined. Adjust seasoning to taste, if needed.
6. Slice the grilled beef tenderloin steaks into smaller pieces to fit the size of the slider buns or dinner rolls.
7. Spread a dollop of horseradish cream on the bottom half of each slider bun or dinner roll.

8. Place a piece of grilled beef tenderloin on top of the horseradish cream.
9. Top with baby arugula or lettuce leaves, sliced tomatoes, and thinly sliced red onions.
10. If desired, sprinkle crispy fried onions over the toppings for added crunch.
11. Place the top halves of the slider buns or dinner rolls over the fillings to form sliders.
12. Garnish with fresh parsley or chives, if using.
13. Serve the Beef Tenderloin Sliders with Horseradish Cream immediately, and enjoy!

These sliders are perfect for parties, gatherings, or as a delicious appetizer. Adjust the toppings and condiments to suit your taste preferences.

Smoked Gouda and Apple Butter on Multigrain Bread

Ingredients:

- 8 slices of multigrain bread
- 8 oz smoked Gouda cheese, thinly sliced
- 1/2 cup apple butter
- Butter, softened, for spreading

Instructions:

1. Preheat a skillet or griddle over medium heat.
2. Lay out the slices of multigrain bread on a clean surface.
3. Spread a thin layer of softened butter on one side of each slice of bread.
4. Place the bread slices butter side down on the preheated skillet or griddle.
5. Layer thinly sliced smoked Gouda cheese on four slices of bread.
6. Spread a generous amount of apple butter on the remaining four slices of bread.
7. Carefully place the apple butter slices of bread on top of the cheese slices to form sandwiches.
8. Cook the sandwiches for 3-4 minutes on each side, or until the bread is golden brown and crispy, and the cheese is melted.
9. Remove the sandwiches from the skillet or griddle and let cool for a minute before serving.
10. Slice the Smoked Gouda and Apple Butter on Multigrain Bread sandwiches in half diagonally before serving, if desired.
11. Serve warm and enjoy the delightful combination of flavors!

This sandwich is perfect for a quick and satisfying lunch or snack, combining the smoky richness of Gouda cheese with the sweet and tangy flavor of apple butter on wholesome multigrain bread.

California Club Sandwich with Avocado and Bacon

Ingredients:

- 8 slices of your favorite sandwich bread (such as whole wheat or sourdough)
- 8 slices of cooked bacon
- 2 ripe avocados, sliced
- 1 large tomato, thinly sliced
- 4 leaves of green leaf lettuce
- 4 slices of cooked turkey or chicken breast
- Mayonnaise
- Dijon mustard (optional)
- Salt and pepper to taste

Instructions:

1. Toast the slices of bread until golden brown.
2. Spread mayonnaise on one side of each slice of bread.
3. If desired, spread Dijon mustard on the other side of each slice of bread.
4. Layer the sandwich ingredients on four slices of bread in the following order: green leaf lettuce, sliced tomato, cooked bacon, sliced avocado, and cooked turkey or chicken breast.
5. Season the avocado slices with salt and pepper to taste.
6. Place the remaining slices of bread on top to form sandwiches.
7. Cut each sandwich in half diagonally.
8. Serve the California Club Sandwiches immediately and enjoy!

This sandwich is a delicious combination of flavors and textures, perfect for a quick and satisfying meal. Feel free to customize the ingredients to suit your taste preferences.

Pulled BBQ Jackfruit Sandwich with Slaw

Ingredients:

For the Pulled BBQ Jackfruit:

- 2 cans young green jackfruit in water or brine, drained and rinsed
- 1 tablespoon olive oil
- 1 small onion, finely chopped
- 2 cloves garlic, minced
- 1 cup barbecue sauce
- 1/2 cup vegetable broth or water
- Salt and pepper to taste

For the Slaw:

- 2 cups shredded cabbage (green or purple)
- 1 carrot, grated
- 2 green onions, thinly sliced
- 1/4 cup mayonnaise
- 1 tablespoon apple cider vinegar
- 1 tablespoon honey or maple syrup
- Salt and pepper to taste

For Serving:

- Hamburger buns or sandwich rolls
- Additional barbecue sauce (optional)
- Pickles (optional)

Instructions:

1. Heat olive oil in a large skillet over medium heat. Add chopped onion and garlic, and sauté until softened, about 2-3 minutes.
2. Add drained and rinsed jackfruit to the skillet. Using a fork, break up the jackfruit into smaller pieces resembling pulled pork.
3. Add barbecue sauce and vegetable broth (or water) to the skillet. Stir to combine.
4. Reduce heat to low and simmer, uncovered, for 15-20 minutes, or until the jackfruit is tender and the sauce has thickened. Use a fork to continue breaking up the jackfruit as it cooks.

5. While the jackfruit is cooking, prepare the slaw. In a large mixing bowl, combine shredded cabbage, grated carrot, and thinly sliced green onions.
6. In a small bowl, whisk together mayonnaise, apple cider vinegar, honey or maple syrup, salt, and pepper to taste.
7. Pour the dressing over the cabbage mixture and toss until well combined. Adjust seasoning to taste, if needed.
8. Once the jackfruit is cooked, assemble the sandwiches. Place a generous portion of the pulled BBQ jackfruit on the bottom half of each hamburger bun or sandwich roll.
9. Top the jackfruit with a spoonful of slaw.
10. If desired, drizzle additional barbecue sauce over the slaw.
11. Place the top half of the hamburger bun or sandwich roll over the fillings to form sandwiches.
12. Serve the Pulled BBQ Jackfruit Sandwiches with Slaw immediately, and enjoy!

These sandwiches are a delicious and satisfying vegetarian alternative to traditional pulled pork sandwiches, with the jackfruit mimicking the texture and flavor of pulled pork. The tangy slaw adds a refreshing crunch to balance the richness of the barbecue jackfruit.

Pesto Chicken Salad Croissant

Ingredients:

For the Pesto Chicken Salad:

- 2 cups cooked chicken breast, shredded or diced
- 1/4 cup basil pesto
- 1/4 cup mayonnaise
- 2 tablespoons plain Greek yogurt (optional)
- 1 tablespoon lemon juice
- Salt and pepper to taste
- 1/4 cup chopped sun-dried tomatoes (optional)
- 1/4 cup chopped roasted red peppers (optional)
- 1/4 cup chopped toasted almonds (optional)
- 2 tablespoons chopped fresh basil (optional)

For Serving:

- Croissants, sliced in half
- Lettuce leaves
- Sliced tomatoes
- Sliced red onions
- Avocado slices
- Additional basil leaves for garnish (optional)

Instructions:

1. In a large mixing bowl, combine the cooked chicken breast, basil pesto, mayonnaise, Greek yogurt (if using), lemon juice, salt, and pepper. Stir until well combined and the chicken is evenly coated with the pesto mixture.
2. If using, add the chopped sun-dried tomatoes, roasted red peppers, toasted almonds, and chopped fresh basil to the chicken salad mixture. Stir to incorporate.
3. Taste the chicken salad and adjust seasoning if needed.
4. To assemble the croissants, place a lettuce leaf on the bottom half of each croissant.
5. Spoon a generous portion of the pesto chicken salad on top of the lettuce.
6. Top the chicken salad with sliced tomatoes, sliced red onions, and avocado slices.
7. Add additional basil leaves for garnish, if desired.

8. Place the top half of each croissant over the fillings to form sandwiches.
9. Serve the Pesto Chicken Salad Croissants immediately, and enjoy!

These sandwiches are perfect for a light and refreshing lunch or brunch, with the vibrant flavors of basil pesto complementing the tender chicken perfectly. Feel free to customize the chicken salad with your favorite add-ins and toppings.

Grilled Peach and Prosciutto on Baguette

Ingredients:

- 2 ripe peaches, pitted and sliced into wedges
- 4 slices of prosciutto
- 1 baguette, sliced into 4 pieces and halved lengthwise
- 1 tablespoon olive oil
- Balsamic glaze or reduction (optional)
- Fresh basil leaves for garnish (optional)
- Salt and pepper to taste

Instructions:

1. Preheat a grill or grill pan over medium-high heat.
2. Brush the peach wedges with olive oil and sprinkle with a pinch of salt and pepper.
3. Grill the peach wedges for 2-3 minutes on each side, or until grill marks appear and the peaches are slightly softened. Remove from the grill and set aside.
4. Place the baguette slices on the grill and toast for 1-2 minutes on each side, or until lightly golden and crispy.
5. To assemble the sandwiches, place a slice of prosciutto on the bottom half of each baguette piece.
6. Top the prosciutto with grilled peach wedges.
7. If desired, drizzle balsamic glaze or reduction over the grilled peaches for extra flavor.
8. Garnish with fresh basil leaves, if using.
9. Place the top half of each baguette piece over the fillings to form sandwiches.
10. Serve the Grilled Peach and Prosciutto on Baguette sandwiches immediately, and enjoy!

These sandwiches are a delightful combination of sweet, salty, and savory flavors, with the juicy grilled peaches complementing the rich and savory prosciutto perfectly. Feel free to customize the sandwiches with additional toppings or condiments, such as goat cheese or arugula, to suit your taste preferences.

Spicy Tofu Banh Mi with Sriracha Mayo

Ingredients:

For the Spicy Tofu:

- 1 block extra firm tofu, pressed and sliced into strips
- 2 tablespoons soy sauce
- 1 tablespoon rice vinegar
- 1 tablespoon sesame oil
- 1 tablespoon Sriracha sauce (adjust to taste)
- 1 tablespoon maple syrup or honey
- 2 cloves garlic, minced
- 1 teaspoon grated ginger
- Salt and pepper to taste
- 1 tablespoon vegetable oil, for cooking

For the Sriracha Mayo:

- 1/4 cup mayonnaise
- 1 tablespoon Sriracha sauce (adjust to taste)
- 1 teaspoon lime juice
- Salt to taste

For Serving:

- Baguette or French rolls, sliced lengthwise
- Thinly sliced cucumber
- Thinly sliced carrot
- Thinly sliced jalapeño peppers
- Fresh cilantro leaves
- Thinly sliced red onion
- Pickled daikon and carrot (optional)

Instructions:

1. Preheat your oven to 400°F (200°C). Line a baking sheet with parchment paper.
2. In a bowl, whisk together soy sauce, rice vinegar, sesame oil, Sriracha sauce, maple syrup or honey, minced garlic, grated ginger, salt, and pepper to make the marinade.

3. Place the tofu slices in a shallow dish and pour the marinade over them. Let them marinate for at least 15-20 minutes, flipping them halfway through.
4. Transfer the marinated tofu slices onto the prepared baking sheet. Bake in the preheated oven for 20-25 minutes, flipping halfway through, until the tofu is golden brown and slightly crispy.
5. While the tofu is baking, prepare the Sriracha mayo. In a small bowl, mix together mayonnaise, Sriracha sauce, lime juice, and salt. Adjust the Sriracha sauce to taste.
6. Once the tofu is ready, heat vegetable oil in a skillet over medium-high heat. Add the baked tofu slices and cook for 2-3 minutes on each side until they are crispy.
7. To assemble the banh mi sandwiches, spread Sriracha mayo on one side of each baguette or French roll.
8. Place a few slices of crispy tofu on the bottom half of each roll.
9. Top the tofu with sliced cucumber, carrot, jalapeño peppers, cilantro leaves, and red onion.
10. If using, add pickled daikon and carrot on top.
11. Close the sandwiches with the top halves of the rolls.
12. Serve the Spicy Tofu Banh Mi with Sriracha Mayo immediately, and enjoy!

These banh mi sandwiches are packed with flavor and texture, with the spicy tofu and creamy Sriracha mayo creating a perfect balance. Feel free to adjust the toppings and condiments to suit your taste preferences.

Roasted Vegetable and Goat Cheese Ciabatta

Ingredients:

For the Roasted Vegetables:

- 2 bell peppers (red, yellow, or orange), sliced
- 1 zucchini, sliced
- 1 yellow squash, sliced
- 1 red onion, sliced
- 2 tablespoons olive oil
- Salt and pepper to taste
- 2 cloves garlic, minced
- 1 teaspoon dried Italian seasoning

For the Sandwiches:

- 1 ciabatta loaf, sliced horizontally
- 4 oz goat cheese, softened
- Handful of fresh baby spinach leaves
- Balsamic glaze or reduction (optional)
- Fresh basil leaves for garnish (optional)

Instructions:

1. Preheat your oven to 400°F (200°C).
2. In a large mixing bowl, toss the sliced bell peppers, zucchini, yellow squash, and red onion with olive oil, minced garlic, dried Italian seasoning, salt, and pepper until evenly coated.
3. Spread the seasoned vegetables in a single layer on a baking sheet lined with parchment paper.
4. Roast the vegetables in the preheated oven for 20-25 minutes, or until they are tender and slightly caramelized, stirring halfway through.
5. While the vegetables are roasting, slice the ciabatta loaf horizontally and spread goat cheese evenly on both halves.
6. Once the roasted vegetables are done, remove them from the oven and let them cool slightly.
7. Arrange the roasted vegetables on the bottom half of the ciabatta loaf.
8. Top the roasted vegetables with fresh baby spinach leaves.
9. If desired, drizzle balsamic glaze or reduction over the spinach.
10. Place the top half of the ciabatta loaf over the fillings to form a sandwich.

11. Slice the Roasted Vegetable and Goat Cheese Ciabatta into individual portions.
12. Garnish with fresh basil leaves, if using.
13. Serve the sandwiches immediately, and enjoy!

These sandwiches are bursting with flavor from the roasted vegetables and creamy goat cheese, making them a delicious and satisfying meal. Feel free to customize the vegetables based on your preferences or what you have on hand.

BLT with Basil Mayo on Toasted Sourdough

Ingredients:

For the Basil Mayo:

- 1/2 cup mayonnaise
- 1/4 cup fresh basil leaves, finely chopped
- 1 tablespoon lemon juice
- Salt and pepper to taste

For the BLT:

- 8 slices of thick-cut bacon
- 4 slices of sourdough bread
- 2 large tomatoes, sliced
- 4 leaves of lettuce (such as green leaf or romaine)
- Basil Mayo (from the above ingredients)
- Butter, softened, for spreading

Instructions:

1. Preheat your oven to 400°F (200°C).
2. Prepare the Basil Mayo by combining mayonnaise, finely chopped fresh basil leaves, lemon juice, salt, and pepper in a small bowl. Mix until well combined. Set aside.
3. Arrange the bacon slices in a single layer on a baking sheet lined with parchment paper.
4. Bake the bacon in the preheated oven for 15-20 minutes, or until crispy. Remove from the oven and drain on paper towels.
5. While the bacon is cooking, toast the sourdough bread slices. You can use a toaster or toast them in a skillet over medium heat until golden brown.
6. Spread a generous amount of softened butter on one side of each toasted sourdough bread slice.
7. Spread Basil Mayo on the other side of each bread slice.
8. Arrange the sliced tomatoes on half of the bread slices.
9. Place two lettuce leaves on top of the tomatoes on each slice.
10. Divide the crispy bacon slices evenly among the sandwiches, placing them on top of the lettuce.
11. Top each sandwich with the remaining bread slices, Basil Mayo side down.
12. Slice the BLT sandwiches diagonally, if desired.

13. Serve the BLT with Basil Mayo on Toasted Sourdough immediately, and enjoy!

These sandwiches are a classic combination of crispy bacon, juicy tomatoes, fresh lettuce, and creamy Basil Mayo, all nestled between slices of toasted sourdough bread. They're perfect for a satisfying lunch or brunch. Feel free to customize the ingredients or add extras like avocado slices or a fried egg to suit your taste preferences.

Crab Cake Sandwich with Old Bay Aioli

Ingredients:

For the Crab Cakes:

- 1 lb lump crab meat, drained
- 1/4 cup mayonnaise
- 1 egg
- 1 tablespoon Dijon mustard
- 1 tablespoon Worcestershire sauce
- 1 tablespoon lemon juice
- 1/4 cup breadcrumbs
- 2 green onions, finely chopped
- 1/4 cup chopped fresh parsley
- Salt and pepper to taste
- 1/4 cup flour (for dredging)
- 2 tablespoons olive oil (for frying)

For the Old Bay Aioli:

- 1/2 cup mayonnaise
- 1 tablespoon lemon juice
- 1 teaspoon Old Bay seasoning
- 1 clove garlic, minced
- Salt and pepper to taste

For Serving:

- Sandwich buns or rolls
- Lettuce leaves
- Sliced tomatoes
- Sliced red onion
- Pickles (optional)

Instructions:

1. In a large mixing bowl, combine lump crab meat, mayonnaise, egg, Dijon mustard, Worcestershire sauce, lemon juice, breadcrumbs, chopped green onions, chopped fresh parsley, salt, and pepper. Gently mix until well combined, being careful not to break up the crab meat too much.

2. Divide the crab mixture into equal portions and shape each portion into a patty.
3. Dredge each crab cake in flour, shaking off any excess.
4. Heat olive oil in a skillet over medium-high heat. Once the oil is hot, add the crab cakes to the skillet and cook for 3-4 minutes on each side, or until golden brown and crispy. Transfer the cooked crab cakes to a plate lined with paper towels to drain any excess oil.
5. While the crab cakes are cooking, prepare the Old Bay aioli. In a small bowl, combine mayonnaise, lemon juice, Old Bay seasoning, minced garlic, salt, and pepper. Mix until well combined. Adjust seasoning to taste, if needed.
6. To assemble the sandwiches, spread a generous amount of Old Bay aioli on the bottom half of each sandwich bun or roll.
7. Place a lettuce leaf on top of the aioli.
8. Arrange a sliced tomato and sliced red onion on top of the lettuce.
9. Place a cooked crab cake on top of the vegetables.
10. If desired, add pickles on top of the crab cake.
11. Place the top half of each sandwich bun or roll over the fillings to form sandwiches.
12. Serve the Crab Cake Sandwiches with Old Bay Aioli immediately, and enjoy!

These sandwiches are a delicious combination of crispy crab cakes and flavorful Old Bay aioli, perfect for a summery lunch or dinner. Feel free to customize the toppings and condiments to suit your taste preferences.

Turkey Reuben with Coleslaw and Swiss Cheese

Ingredients:

For the Coleslaw:

- 2 cups shredded cabbage (green or purple)
- 1 carrot, grated
- 2 green onions, thinly sliced
- 1/4 cup mayonnaise
- 1 tablespoon apple cider vinegar
- 1 teaspoon honey or maple syrup
- Salt and pepper to taste

For the Turkey Reuben:

- 8 slices rye bread
- 8 slices Swiss cheese
- 1 lb thinly sliced turkey breast
- 1/2 cup sauerkraut, drained
- 1/4 cup thousand island dressing
- Butter, softened, for spreading

Instructions:

1. Preheat a skillet or griddle over medium heat.
2. In a large mixing bowl, combine shredded cabbage, grated carrot, thinly sliced green onions, mayonnaise, apple cider vinegar, honey or maple syrup, salt, and pepper to taste. Mix until well combined to make the coleslaw. Set aside.
3. Spread softened butter on one side of each slice of rye bread.
4. Place the bread slices butter side down on the preheated skillet or griddle.
5. Top four of the bread slices with a slice of Swiss cheese.
6. Add a layer of thinly sliced turkey breast on top of the cheese on each slice.
7. Top the turkey with a spoonful of drained sauerkraut on each slice.
8. Drizzle a spoonful of thousand island dressing over the sauerkraut on each slice.
9. Spread a generous portion of coleslaw over the remaining four bread slices.
10. Once the cheese has melted and the bread is golden brown on the bottom, carefully place the coleslaw-topped bread slices over the turkey and sauerkraut to form sandwiches.
11. Use a spatula to press down gently on each sandwich.

12. Cook for another 2-3 minutes, or until the bottom of the sandwiches is golden brown and crispy.
13. Carefully flip the sandwiches and cook for another 2-3 minutes on the other side, or until golden brown and the cheese is melted.
14. Remove the Turkey Reuben with Coleslaw and Swiss Cheese sandwiches from the skillet or griddle and let them cool for a minute before serving.
15. Slice the sandwiches in half diagonally before serving, if desired.
16. Serve hot and enjoy your delicious Turkey Reuben sandwiches with a side of pickles or potato chips!

These sandwiches are a flavorful twist on the classic Reuben, with juicy turkey, tangy sauerkraut, creamy coleslaw, and melted Swiss cheese all nestled between slices of toasted rye bread.

Grilled Halloumi and Vegetable Wrap with Tzatziki

Ingredients:

For the Tzatziki:

- 1 cup Greek yogurt
- 1/2 cucumber, grated and squeezed to remove excess moisture
- 2 cloves garlic, minced
- 1 tablespoon fresh lemon juice
- 1 tablespoon extra virgin olive oil
- 1 tablespoon chopped fresh dill (or mint)
- Salt and pepper to taste

For the Grilled Halloumi and Vegetables:

- 1 block halloumi cheese, sliced
- 1 red bell pepper, sliced
- 1 yellow bell pepper, sliced
- 1 zucchini, sliced lengthwise
- 1 yellow squash, sliced lengthwise
- 1 red onion, sliced
- 2 tablespoons olive oil
- Salt and pepper to taste
- 4 large flour tortillas or wraps

For Serving:

- Fresh spinach or arugula leaves
- Sliced tomatoes
- Sliced cucumbers
- Sliced red onion
- Fresh parsley or dill for garnish (optional)

Instructions:

1. Prepare the Tzatziki by combining Greek yogurt, grated cucumber, minced garlic, lemon juice, olive oil, chopped fresh dill, salt, and pepper in a bowl. Stir until well combined. Adjust seasoning to taste, cover, and refrigerate until ready to use.
2. Preheat a grill or grill pan over medium-high heat.

3. In a large mixing bowl, toss the sliced bell peppers, zucchini, yellow squash, and red onion with olive oil, salt, and pepper until evenly coated.
4. Grill the vegetables on the preheated grill for 3-4 minutes on each side, or until tender and slightly charred. Remove from the grill and set aside.
5. Grill the halloumi cheese slices on the preheated grill for 1-2 minutes on each side, or until grill marks appear and the cheese is softened.
6. To assemble the wraps, spread a generous amount of tzatziki sauce on each flour tortilla or wrap.
7. Place a few grilled halloumi slices on top of the tzatziki sauce on each wrap.
8. Arrange the grilled vegetables on top of the halloumi slices.
9. Add a handful of fresh spinach or arugula leaves, sliced tomatoes, sliced cucumbers, and sliced red onion on top of the vegetables.
10. Garnish with fresh parsley or dill, if using.
11. Roll up the wraps tightly and slice them in half diagonally before serving, if desired.
12. Serve the Grilled Halloumi and Vegetable Wraps with Tzatziki immediately, and enjoy!

These wraps are packed with flavor and freshness, making them a delicious and satisfying meal. Feel free to customize the vegetables and add extra toppings or condiments to suit your taste preferences.

Roast Beef and Gorgonzola on Rye

Ingredients:

- 8 slices of rye bread
- 1 lb thinly sliced roast beef
- 4 oz Gorgonzola cheese, crumbled
- 1/2 cup caramelized onions
- 1/4 cup mayonnaise
- 2 tablespoons Dijon mustard
- Fresh arugula or spinach leaves
- Butter, softened, for spreading

Instructions:

1. Preheat a skillet or panini press over medium heat.
2. In a small bowl, mix together mayonnaise and Dijon mustard until well combined.
3. Spread the mayonnaise mixture evenly on one side of each slice of rye bread.
4. Layer thinly sliced roast beef on four slices of the rye bread.
5. Sprinkle crumbled Gorgonzola cheese over the roast beef on each slice.
6. Top with caramelized onions.
7. Place a handful of fresh arugula or spinach leaves on top of the onions.
8. Place the remaining four slices of rye bread on top to form sandwiches.
9. Spread softened butter on the outer side of each sandwich.
10. Place the sandwiches in the preheated skillet or panini press.
11. Cook for 3-4 minutes on each side, or until the bread is golden brown and crispy, and the cheese is melted.
12. Remove the sandwiches from the skillet or panini press and let them cool for a minute before serving.
13. Slice the Roast Beef and Gorgonzola on Rye sandwiches in half diagonally before serving, if desired.
14. Serve hot and enjoy your delicious sandwiches!

These sandwiches are rich and flavorful, with the tangy Gorgonzola cheese complementing the savory roast beef and sweet caramelized onions perfectly. Feel free to adjust the ingredients or add extra toppings to suit your taste preferences.

Veggie Burger with Caramelized Onions and Smoked Gouda

Ingredients:

For the Veggie Patties:

- 2 cups cooked quinoa or brown rice
- 1 can (15 oz) black beans, drained and rinsed
- 1 cup cooked sweet potato, mashed
- 1/2 cup bread crumbs
- 1/4 cup chopped onion
- 2 cloves garlic, minced
- 1 teaspoon ground cumin
- 1 teaspoon paprika
- Salt and pepper to taste
- 2 tablespoons olive oil, for cooking

For the Caramelized Onions:

- 2 large onions, thinly sliced
- 2 tablespoons olive oil
- 1 tablespoon balsamic vinegar
- Salt and pepper to taste

For Serving:

- Smoked Gouda cheese slices
- Burger buns
- Lettuce leaves
- Sliced tomatoes
- Pickles (optional)
- Your favorite burger condiments (such as mayo, ketchup, or mustard)

Instructions:

1. Start by making the caramelized onions. Heat olive oil in a skillet over medium-low heat. Add the thinly sliced onions and cook, stirring occasionally, until they are soft and golden brown, about 20-25 minutes.
2. Once the onions are caramelized, stir in balsamic vinegar and season with salt and pepper. Cook for another 2-3 minutes, then remove from heat and set aside.

3. In a large mixing bowl, mash the black beans with a fork or potato masher until they form a chunky paste.
4. Add cooked quinoa or brown rice, mashed sweet potato, chopped onion, minced garlic, bread crumbs, ground cumin, paprika, salt, and pepper to the bowl with the mashed black beans. Mix until all ingredients are well combined.
5. Divide the mixture into equal portions and shape each portion into a patty.
6. Heat olive oil in a skillet over medium heat. Once the oil is hot, add the veggie patties to the skillet and cook for 4-5 minutes on each side, or until they are golden brown and crispy.
7. During the last minute of cooking, place a slice of smoked Gouda cheese on top of each veggie patty and cover the skillet with a lid to allow the cheese to melt.
8. To assemble the burgers, place lettuce leaves on the bottom half of each burger bun.
9. Top with a veggie patty topped with melted smoked Gouda cheese.
10. Add a spoonful of caramelized onions on top of the cheese.
11. Add sliced tomatoes and pickles, if desired.
12. Spread your favorite burger condiments on the top half of each burger bun.
13. Place the top half of each burger bun over the fillings to complete the burgers.
14. Serve the Veggie Burgers with Caramelized Onions and Smoked Gouda immediately, and enjoy!

These veggie burgers are packed with flavor and texture, with the sweetness of the caramelized onions and the smoky richness of the smoked Gouda cheese complementing the hearty veggie patties perfectly. Feel free to customize the toppings and condiments to suit your taste preferences.

Chicken Gyro with Tzatziki Sauce

Ingredients:

For the Chicken Gyro:

- 1 lb boneless, skinless chicken breasts or thighs, thinly sliced
- 2 tablespoons olive oil
- 2 cloves garlic, minced
- 1 tablespoon lemon juice
- 1 teaspoon dried oregano
- 1 teaspoon paprika
- Salt and pepper to taste
- Pita bread or flatbreads
- Sliced tomatoes
- Sliced red onions
- Sliced cucumbers
- Fresh parsley or dill for garnish (optional)

For the Tzatziki Sauce:

- 1 cup Greek yogurt
- 1/2 cucumber, grated and squeezed to remove excess moisture
- 2 cloves garlic, minced
- 1 tablespoon fresh lemon juice
- 1 tablespoon extra virgin olive oil
- 1 tablespoon chopped fresh dill (or mint)
- Salt and pepper to taste

Instructions:

1. In a mixing bowl, combine olive oil, minced garlic, lemon juice, dried oregano, paprika, salt, and pepper. Add the thinly sliced chicken and toss until well coated. Cover and marinate in the refrigerator for at least 30 minutes, or overnight for best flavor.
2. While the chicken is marinating, prepare the tzatziki sauce. In a bowl, combine Greek yogurt, grated cucumber, minced garlic, lemon juice, extra virgin olive oil, chopped fresh dill, salt, and pepper. Mix until well combined. Adjust seasoning to taste, cover, and refrigerate until ready to use.

3. Preheat a grill or grill pan over medium-high heat. Once hot, add the marinated chicken slices and cook for 4-5 minutes on each side, or until cooked through and slightly charred. Remove from heat and let it rest for a few minutes.
4. Warm the pita bread or flatbreads on the grill for a minute on each side.
5. To assemble the gyros, spread a generous amount of tzatziki sauce on each warmed pita bread or flatbread.
6. Top with slices of grilled chicken.
7. Add sliced tomatoes, red onions, and cucumbers on top of the chicken.
8. Garnish with fresh parsley or dill, if using.
9. Fold the pita bread or flatbread over the fillings to form a gyro.
10. Serve the Chicken Gyros with Tzatziki Sauce immediately, and enjoy!

These chicken gyros are flavorful and satisfying, with tender grilled chicken, crisp vegetables, and creamy tzatziki sauce wrapped in warm pita bread. Feel free to customize the toppings and add extras like feta cheese, olives, or hot sauce to suit your taste preferences.

Pear, Gouda, and Bacon Panini

Ingredients:

- 4 slices of bread (sourdough, ciabatta, or any hearty bread of your choice)
- 4 oz Gouda cheese, thinly sliced
- 1 ripe pear, thinly sliced
- 4 slices of cooked bacon
- Butter, softened, for spreading

Instructions:

1. Preheat a panini press or a skillet over medium heat.
2. Lay out the slices of bread on a clean surface.
3. Place slices of Gouda cheese on two slices of bread.
4. Top the cheese with slices of ripe pear.
5. Place slices of cooked bacon on top of the pear.
6. Close the sandwiches with the remaining slices of bread.
7. Spread a thin layer of softened butter on the outer sides of the sandwiches.
8. Place the sandwiches on the preheated panini press or skillet.
9. If using a panini press, close the lid and cook for 4-5 minutes, or until the bread is golden brown and the cheese is melted.
10. If using a skillet, place a heavy pan or a heatproof plate on top of the sandwiches to press them down. Cook for 2-3 minutes on each side, or until the bread is golden brown and the cheese is melted, flipping halfway through.
11. Once the sandwiches are cooked to your liking, remove them from the panini press or skillet.
12. Let them cool for a minute before slicing them in half diagonally.
13. Serve the Pear, Gouda, and Bacon Panini immediately, and enjoy!

These panini are a delicious combination of sweet, salty, and savory flavors, with the creamy Gouda cheese complementing the sweetness of the ripe pear and the smoky saltiness of the bacon. Feel free to customize the sandwiches by adding a spread like Dijon mustard or honey, or by using different types of bread or cheese.

Smoked Salmon and Avocado Toasted Bagel

Ingredients:

- 2 bagels, sliced and toasted
- 4 oz smoked salmon
- 1 ripe avocado, sliced
- 2 tablespoons cream cheese (optional)
- Red onion, thinly sliced (optional)
- Capers (optional)
- Fresh dill or chives, chopped (optional)
- Lemon wedges, for serving

Instructions:

1. Toast the bagel halves until golden brown and crispy.
2. If using, spread cream cheese on each toasted bagel half.
3. Place slices of smoked salmon on top of the cream cheese (if using) or directly on the toasted bagel halves.
4. Arrange slices of ripe avocado on top of the smoked salmon.
5. If desired, top with thinly sliced red onion and capers.
6. Garnish with chopped fresh dill or chives, if using.
7. Serve the Smoked Salmon and Avocado Toasted Bagel immediately, with lemon wedges on the side for squeezing over the top.
8. Enjoy your delicious and satisfying breakfast or brunch!

This Smoked Salmon and Avocado Toasted Bagel is a classic combination of flavors and textures, with the richness of the smoked salmon and creamy avocado complementing the crispy toasted bagel perfectly. Feel free to customize the toppings to suit your taste preferences, and add extras like tomato slices or arugula for extra freshness.

Roast Lamb Sandwich with Mint Aioli

Ingredients:

For the Roast Lamb:

- 1 lb boneless leg of lamb
- 2 cloves garlic, minced
- 2 tablespoons olive oil
- 1 tablespoon lemon juice
- 1 teaspoon dried rosemary
- 1 teaspoon dried thyme
- Salt and pepper to taste

For the Mint Aioli:

- 1/2 cup mayonnaise
- 2 tablespoons chopped fresh mint leaves
- 1 clove garlic, minced
- 1 tablespoon lemon juice
- Salt and pepper to taste

For Serving:

- Sandwich bread or rolls (such as ciabatta or focaccia)
- Lettuce leaves
- Sliced tomatoes
- Sliced red onion

Instructions:

1. Preheat your oven to 375°F (190°C).
2. In a small bowl, combine minced garlic, olive oil, lemon juice, dried rosemary, dried thyme, salt, and pepper to make the marinade for the lamb.
3. Place the boneless leg of lamb in a roasting pan and rub the marinade all over the lamb, making sure it's evenly coated.
4. Roast the lamb in the preheated oven for about 25-30 minutes per pound, or until it reaches your desired level of doneness. The internal temperature should reach 145°F (63°C) for medium-rare, or adjust according to your preference.

5. While the lamb is roasting, prepare the mint aioli. In a small bowl, mix together mayonnaise, chopped fresh mint leaves, minced garlic, lemon juice, salt, and pepper until well combined. Adjust seasoning to taste.
6. Once the lamb is cooked to your liking, remove it from the oven and let it rest for a few minutes before slicing thinly.
7. To assemble the sandwiches, spread a generous amount of mint aioli on each slice of sandwich bread or roll.
8. Layer slices of roasted lamb on the bottom half of each sandwich.
9. Top the lamb with lettuce leaves, sliced tomatoes, and sliced red onion.
10. Place the top half of each sandwich bread or roll over the fillings to form sandwiches.
11. Serve the Roast Lamb Sandwiches with Mint Aioli immediately, and enjoy!

These sandwiches are a delightful combination of tender roasted lamb, fresh vegetables, and flavorful mint aioli, making them perfect for a satisfying lunch or dinner. Feel free to customize the sandwiches with additional toppings or condiments to suit your taste preferences.

Portobello Mushroom Reuben with Russian Dressing

Ingredients:

For the Portobello Mushrooms:

- 4 large Portobello mushroom caps
- 2 tablespoons olive oil
- 2 tablespoons balsamic vinegar
- Salt and pepper to taste

For the Russian Dressing:

- 1/2 cup mayonnaise
- 2 tablespoons ketchup
- 1 tablespoon sweet pickle relish
- 1 teaspoon Worcestershire sauce
- 1 teaspoon Dijon mustard
- Salt and pepper to taste

For Assembling the Sandwiches:

- 8 slices rye bread
- 4 slices Swiss cheese
- Sauerkraut, drained
- Butter, softened, for spreading

Instructions:

1. Preheat the oven to 400°F (200°C).
2. Clean the Portobello mushroom caps and remove the stems.
3. In a small bowl, whisk together olive oil, balsamic vinegar, salt, and pepper.
4. Brush the mushroom caps with the olive oil mixture, coating both sides.
5. Place the mushroom caps on a baking sheet lined with parchment paper.
6. Roast the mushrooms in the preheated oven for about 15-20 minutes, or until they are tender and juicy.
7. While the mushrooms are roasting, prepare the Russian dressing. In a small bowl, mix together mayonnaise, ketchup, sweet pickle relish, Worcestershire sauce, Dijon mustard, salt, and pepper until well combined. Adjust seasoning to taste.
8. Once the mushrooms are cooked, remove them from the oven and let them cool slightly.

9. Spread softened butter on one side of each slice of rye bread.
10. Place the bread slices, buttered side down, on a skillet or griddle over medium heat.
11. Top each bread slice with a slice of Swiss cheese.
12. Add a generous portion of sauerkraut on top of the cheese.
13. Place a roasted Portobello mushroom cap on top of the sauerkraut on each sandwich.
14. Spread a dollop of Russian dressing on the other side of each bread slice.
15. Once the cheese has melted and the bread is toasted, carefully close each sandwich by placing the Russian dressing side on top of the mushroom.
16. Cook for another 1-2 minutes on each side, pressing down gently with a spatula, until the bread is golden brown and crispy.
17. Remove the Portobello Mushroom Reuben sandwiches from the skillet or griddle and let them cool for a minute before serving.
18. Serve the sandwiches hot, and enjoy!

These Portobello Mushroom Reuben sandwiches are a delicious vegetarian twist on the classic Reuben, with meaty mushrooms, tangy sauerkraut, melty Swiss cheese, and creamy Russian dressing all sandwiched between slices of toasted rye bread.

Grilled Chicken and Fig Jam on Brioche

Ingredients:

For the Grilled Chicken:

- 2 boneless, skinless chicken breasts
- 2 tablespoons olive oil
- Salt and pepper to taste

For the Fig Jam:

- 1 cup fresh figs, stems removed and chopped
- 2 tablespoons honey
- 1 tablespoon balsamic vinegar
- Pinch of salt

For Assembling the Sandwiches:

- 4 brioche buns, halved
- 4 slices provolone or Gruyere cheese
- Baby arugula or mixed greens

Instructions:

1. Preheat your grill or grill pan to medium-high heat.
2. Season the chicken breasts with olive oil, salt, and pepper.
3. Grill the chicken breasts for about 6-8 minutes per side, or until they are cooked through and have nice grill marks. Remove from the grill and let them rest for a few minutes before slicing.
4. While the chicken is grilling, prepare the fig jam. In a small saucepan, combine the chopped figs, honey, balsamic vinegar, and a pinch of salt. Cook over medium heat, stirring occasionally, until the figs break down and the mixture thickens into a jam-like consistency, about 8-10 minutes. Remove from heat and let it cool slightly.
5. To assemble the sandwiches, spread a generous amount of fig jam on the bottom half of each brioche bun.
6. Top each bun with a grilled chicken breast.
7. Place a slice of provolone or Gruyere cheese on top of each chicken breast.
8. Add a handful of baby arugula or mixed greens on top of the cheese.

9. Place the top half of each brioche bun over the fillings to complete the sandwiches.
10. Serve the Grilled Chicken and Fig Jam on Brioche sandwiches immediately, and enjoy!

These sandwiches are a delightful combination of savory grilled chicken, sweet and tangy fig jam, melty cheese, and buttery brioche buns. They make for a delicious and satisfying meal, perfect for lunch or dinner. Feel free to customize the sandwiches by adding extras like caramelized onions or crispy bacon, if desired.

Buffalo Cauliflower Wrap with Blue Cheese Dressing

Ingredients:

For the Buffalo Cauliflower:

- 1 head cauliflower, cut into florets
- 1/2 cup all-purpose flour
- 1/2 cup milk (or plant-based milk)
- 1 teaspoon garlic powder
- 1 teaspoon paprika
- Salt and pepper to taste
- 1/2 cup buffalo sauce
- 2 tablespoons melted butter (or olive oil)

For the Blue Cheese Dressing:

- 1/2 cup Greek yogurt (or sour cream)
- 1/4 cup crumbled blue cheese
- 1 tablespoon lemon juice
- 1 tablespoon chopped fresh parsley (optional)
- Salt and pepper to taste

For Assembling the Wraps:

- 4 large flour tortillas or wraps
- Shredded lettuce
- Sliced tomatoes
- Sliced red onion
- Additional buffalo sauce (optional, for extra heat)

Instructions:

1. Preheat your oven to 425°F (220°C). Line a baking sheet with parchment paper or lightly grease it with cooking spray.
2. In a large bowl, whisk together flour, milk, garlic powder, paprika, salt, and pepper until you have a smooth batter.
3. Add cauliflower florets to the batter, tossing until they are evenly coated.
4. Spread the coated cauliflower florets in a single layer on the prepared baking sheet.

5. Bake in the preheated oven for 20-25 minutes, or until the cauliflower is golden brown and crispy.
6. While the cauliflower is baking, prepare the blue cheese dressing. In a small bowl, mix together Greek yogurt (or sour cream), crumbled blue cheese, lemon juice, chopped fresh parsley (if using), salt, and pepper until well combined. Adjust seasoning to taste.
7. Once the cauliflower is cooked, remove it from the oven and transfer it to a large bowl.
8. Drizzle melted butter (or olive oil) and buffalo sauce over the baked cauliflower florets, tossing until they are evenly coated.
9. To assemble the wraps, spread a generous amount of blue cheese dressing on each flour tortilla or wrap.
10. Top with shredded lettuce, sliced tomatoes, and sliced red onion.
11. Place a portion of the buffalo cauliflower on top of the vegetables on each wrap.
12. Drizzle with additional buffalo sauce, if desired, for extra heat.
13. Roll up the wraps tightly and slice them in half diagonally before serving, if desired.
14. Serve the Buffalo Cauliflower Wraps with Blue Cheese Dressing immediately, and enjoy!

These wraps are a delicious and healthier alternative to traditional buffalo chicken wraps, with crispy baked cauliflower florets coated in spicy buffalo sauce and creamy blue cheese dressing. They make for a satisfying lunch or dinner option, packed with flavor and texture. Feel free to customize the wraps by adding extras like avocado slices or chopped celery for added crunch.

Turkey and Cranberry Chutney on Walnut Bread

Ingredients:

For the Cranberry Chutney:

- 1 cup fresh cranberries
- 1/4 cup water
- 1/4 cup granulated sugar
- 1 tablespoon apple cider vinegar
- 1/4 teaspoon ground cinnamon
- Pinch of salt

For the Sandwich:

- Sliced roasted turkey breast
- Walnut bread (or any hearty bread of your choice)
- Arugula or mixed greens
- Cream cheese (optional)

Instructions:

1. Start by making the cranberry chutney. In a small saucepan, combine fresh cranberries, water, granulated sugar, apple cider vinegar, ground cinnamon, and a pinch of salt.
2. Bring the mixture to a boil over medium heat, then reduce the heat to low and let it simmer for about 10-15 minutes, stirring occasionally, until the cranberries burst and the mixture thickens into a chutney-like consistency.
3. Once the chutney is cooked, remove it from the heat and let it cool slightly.
4. While the cranberry chutney is cooling, prepare the sandwich ingredients. Slice the walnut bread into thick slices.
5. If desired, spread a layer of cream cheese on one side of each slice of walnut bread.
6. Place a generous amount of sliced roasted turkey breast on one slice of walnut bread.
7. Spoon a dollop of cranberry chutney over the turkey.
8. Top with a handful of arugula or mixed greens.
9. Place the other slice of walnut bread on top to complete the sandwich.
10. Repeat with the remaining ingredients to make additional sandwiches.
11. Slice the sandwiches in half diagonally before serving, if desired.

12. Serve the Turkey and Cranberry Chutney on Walnut Bread sandwiches immediately, and enjoy!

These sandwiches are a delicious combination of savory roasted turkey, tangy cranberry chutney, and nutty walnut bread, with a hint of creaminess from the optional cream cheese. They're perfect for using up leftover turkey from holiday dinners or for a tasty and satisfying lunch any time of year. Feel free to customize the sandwiches by adding extras like sliced brie cheese or caramelized onions for extra flavor.

Grilled Asparagus and Pesto Mayo on Sourdough

Ingredients:

For the Grilled Asparagus:

- 1 bunch of asparagus, tough ends trimmed
- 1 tablespoon olive oil
- Salt and pepper to taste

For the Pesto Mayo:

- 1/4 cup mayonnaise
- 2 tablespoons prepared pesto sauce

For the Sandwich:

- Sourdough bread, sliced
- Pesto mayo (from above)
- Grilled asparagus (from above)
- Optional: Sliced tomatoes, arugula, or other greens

Instructions:

1. Preheat your grill or grill pan over medium-high heat.
2. In a bowl, toss the trimmed asparagus with olive oil, salt, and pepper until evenly coated.
3. Place the asparagus on the preheated grill and cook for 4-5 minutes, turning occasionally, until they are tender and have grill marks. Remove from heat and set aside.
4. While the asparagus is grilling, prepare the pesto mayo. In a small bowl, mix together mayonnaise and prepared pesto sauce until well combined. Adjust the amount of pesto to taste.
5. Once the asparagus is grilled and cooled slightly, spread a generous amount of pesto mayo on one side of each slice of sourdough bread.
6. Place a layer of grilled asparagus on one slice of bread.
7. If desired, add additional toppings like sliced tomatoes or arugula.
8. Place the other slice of sourdough bread on top to complete the sandwich.
9. Repeat with the remaining ingredients to make additional sandwiches.
10. Slice the sandwiches in half diagonally before serving, if desired.

11. Serve the Grilled Asparagus and Pesto Mayo on Sourdough sandwiches immediately, and enjoy!

These sandwiches are a delicious and flavorful way to enjoy grilled asparagus, with the added tanginess of the pesto mayo and the hearty texture of sourdough bread. They make for a perfect light lunch or dinner option, especially during the warmer months when asparagus is in season. Feel free to customize the sandwiches with your favorite toppings or additional spreads, such as avocado or hummus, for extra flavor.

Prosciutto, Fig, and Arugula on Baguette

Ingredients:

- 1 baguette, sliced into individual sandwich-sized portions
- Prosciutto slices (1-2 per sandwich, depending on preference)
- Fresh figs, sliced
- Arugula leaves
- Balsamic glaze (optional, for drizzling)
- Extra virgin olive oil (optional, for drizzling)
- Salt and pepper to taste

Instructions:

1. Preheat your oven to 350°F (175°C).
2. If desired, lightly toast the baguette slices in the preheated oven for a few minutes until they are warmed through and slightly crispy.
3. While the baguette slices are toasting, prepare the remaining ingredients.
4. Wash and dry the arugula leaves, and slice the fresh figs.
5. Once the baguette slices are toasted to your liking, remove them from the oven and let them cool slightly.
6. To assemble the sandwiches, layer a few slices of prosciutto on each baguette slice.
7. Top the prosciutto with slices of fresh fig.
8. Add a handful of arugula leaves on top of the figs.
9. If desired, drizzle a little balsamic glaze and/or extra virgin olive oil over the arugula.
10. Season with salt and pepper to taste.
11. Repeat with the remaining baguette slices and ingredients to make additional sandwiches.
12. Serve the Prosciutto, Fig, and Arugula on Baguette sandwiches immediately, and enjoy!

These sandwiches are a delightful combination of sweet and savory flavors, with the saltiness of the prosciutto contrasting beautifully with the sweetness of the fresh figs, and the peppery arugula adding a fresh crunch. They make for a perfect light lunch or appetizer, especially when served alongside a simple salad or soup. Feel free to customize the sandwiches by adding extras like goat cheese or a drizzle of honey for extra richness and flavor.

Smoked Salmon and Cucumber Tea Sandwiches

Ingredients:

- 8 slices of sandwich bread (white, whole wheat, or multigrain)
- 4 oz smoked salmon
- 1 small cucumber, thinly sliced
- 4 oz cream cheese, softened
- 1 tablespoon fresh dill, chopped
- 1 tablespoon lemon juice
- Salt and pepper to taste

Instructions:

1. In a small bowl, mix together the softened cream cheese, chopped fresh dill, lemon juice, salt, and pepper until well combined.
2. Lay out the slices of sandwich bread on a clean surface.
3. Spread a generous layer of the cream cheese mixture on one side of each slice of bread.
4. Arrange slices of smoked salmon on half of the bread slices.
5. Top the smoked salmon with thinly sliced cucumber.
6. Place the remaining slices of bread, cream cheese side down, on top to form sandwiches.
7. Using a sharp knife, trim off the crusts from each sandwich to create neat squares or rectangles.
8. Cut each sandwich into quarters to create tea-sized portions.
9. Arrange the Smoked Salmon and Cucumber Tea Sandwiches on a serving platter.
10. Optionally, garnish with additional dill sprigs or lemon slices for presentation.
11. Serve immediately, and enjoy these elegant and delicious tea sandwiches!

These Smoked Salmon and Cucumber Tea Sandwiches are perfect for a fancy afternoon tea or as an elegant appetizer for any gathering. The combination of creamy cream cheese, smoky salmon, and refreshing cucumber creates a delightful flavor and texture contrast, making these sandwiches a favorite among tea enthusiasts. Feel free to customize the sandwiches by adding thinly sliced red onion, capers, or a squeeze of lemon juice for extra flavor.

Turkey, Apple, and Brie on Cranberry Walnut Bread

Ingredients:

- 8 slices of cranberry walnut bread
- 8 oz sliced turkey breast
- 1 apple, thinly sliced (such as Granny Smith or Honeycrisp)
- 4 oz Brie cheese, sliced
- Dijon mustard (optional)
- Honey (optional)
- Arugula or mixed greens (optional)
- Butter, softened, for spreading (optional)

Instructions:

1. Preheat a panini press or grill pan over medium heat.
2. Lay out the slices of cranberry walnut bread on a clean surface.
3. If desired, spread a thin layer of Dijon mustard or honey on one side of each slice of bread.
4. Layer slices of turkey breast on half of the bread slices.
5. Top the turkey with slices of apple.
6. Place slices of Brie cheese on top of the apple slices.
7. Optionally, add a handful of arugula or mixed greens on top of the Brie.
8. Place the remaining slices of cranberry walnut bread on top to form sandwiches.
9. Spread a thin layer of softened butter on the outer sides of the sandwiches.
10. Place the sandwiches on the preheated panini press or grill pan.
11. If using a panini press, close the lid and cook for 4-5 minutes, or until the bread is golden brown and the cheese is melted.
12. If using a grill pan, cook the sandwiches for 3-4 minutes on each side, pressing down gently with a spatula, until the bread is golden brown and the cheese is melted, flipping halfway through.
13. Once the sandwiches are cooked to your liking, remove them from the panini press or grill pan.
14. Let them cool for a minute before slicing them in half diagonally.
15. Serve the Turkey, Apple, and Brie on Cranberry Walnut Bread sandwiches immediately, and enjoy!

These sandwiches are a delicious combination of savory turkey, sweet and tangy apples, creamy Brie cheese, and nutty cranberry walnut bread, making them perfect for a satisfying lunch or dinner option. Feel free to customize the sandwiches by adding extras like caramelized onions or bacon for extra flavor.

Steak and Caramelized Onion Sandwich with Horseradish Cream

Ingredients:

For the Steak:

- 1 lb steak of your choice (such as sirloin, ribeye, or flank steak)
- Salt and pepper to taste
- Olive oil for cooking

For the Caramelized Onions:

- 2 large onions, thinly sliced
- 2 tablespoons butter
- Salt and pepper to taste

For the Horseradish Cream:

- 1/2 cup sour cream
- 2 tablespoons prepared horseradish
- 1 tablespoon Dijon mustard
- 1 tablespoon fresh lemon juice
- Salt and pepper to taste

For Assembling the Sandwiches:

- Sliced sandwich bread or rolls (such as ciabatta or hoagie rolls)
- Baby spinach or arugula (optional)

Instructions:

1. Preheat your grill or grill pan over medium-high heat.
2. Season the steak generously with salt and pepper on both sides.
3. Drizzle olive oil over the steak and rub it in to coat evenly.
4. Grill the steak for about 4-5 minutes per side, or until it reaches your desired level of doneness. Remove from the grill and let it rest for a few minutes before slicing.
5. While the steak is grilling, prepare the caramelized onions. In a large skillet, melt the butter over medium heat. Add the thinly sliced onions and cook, stirring occasionally, until they are golden brown and caramelized, about 20-25 minutes. Season with salt and pepper to taste.

6. While the onions are caramelizing, prepare the horseradish cream. In a small bowl, mix together the sour cream, prepared horseradish, Dijon mustard, fresh lemon juice, salt, and pepper until well combined. Adjust seasoning to taste.
7. Once the steak is rested, slice it thinly against the grain.
8. To assemble the sandwiches, spread a generous amount of horseradish cream on one side of each slice of sandwich bread or roll.
9. Layer slices of grilled steak on top of the horseradish cream.
10. Top the steak with a generous portion of caramelized onions.
11. If desired, add a handful of baby spinach or arugula on top for extra freshness.
12. Place the other slice of sandwich bread or roll on top to complete the sandwich.
13. Repeat with the remaining ingredients to make additional sandwiches.
14. Serve the Steak and Caramelized Onion Sandwiches with Horseradish Cream immediately, and enjoy!

These sandwiches are a delicious combination of savory grilled steak, sweet and flavorful caramelized onions, and tangy horseradish cream, all sandwiched between slices of bread or rolls. They make for a hearty and satisfying meal, perfect for lunch or dinner. Feel free to customize the sandwiches by adding extras like melted cheese or roasted red peppers for extra flavor.

www.ingramcontent.com/pod-product-compliance
Lightning Source LLC
LaVergne TN
LVHW081612060526
838201LV00054B/2209